Early Years
Activity Book

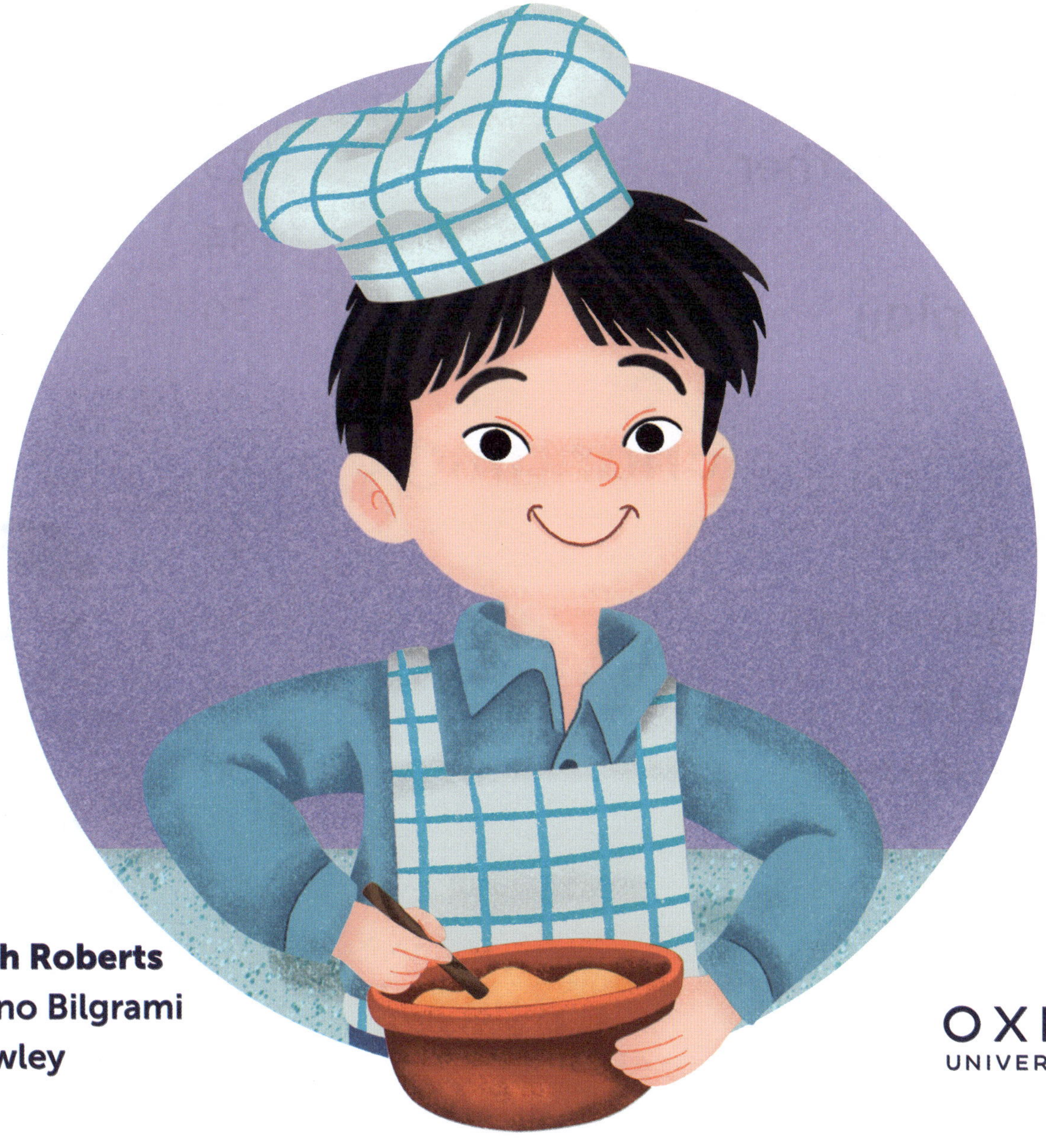

5

Deborah Roberts
Shahbano Bilgrami
Sue Cowley

OXFORD
UNIVERSITY PRESS

Contents

What's cooking? — 3
Making food — 4
Measure and mix — 9
Favourite recipes — 14
Let's all cook! — 19

Rain or shine — 24
Super seasons — 25
Changing weather — 29
Storms — 34
Weather play — 39

Growing and changing — 44
Getting bigger — 45
Plants grow too! — 50
Growing up — 55
Let's measure! — 60

What's cooking?

In this topic, learners are encouraged to:
- arrange directions in the right order
- complete words by adding missing letters
- count and compare things using more/less than
- discuss food preferences
- find rhyming words
- identify pieces of kitchen equipment.

Teachers will also help learners to:
- discover more about world foods
- make simple recipes
- create simple role-plays about food
- recite nursery rhymes related to food
- understand where food comes from.

Making food

Snack time

a Find the child with no snack. How do they feel?

b Retell the story.

At home

Ask your child to be your 'assistant' in the kitchen by counting out the number of ingredients you need to prepare a meal.

In this session, children will also: compare stories on the theme of helping, make a bread and jam snack. → TG pp. 181–184

Making food

a Count the wheat plants.
b Tick (✓) the windmill with 4 sails.

In this session, children will also: investigate flour, learn about cardinal values by counting pasta shapes, act out a story. → TG pp. 181–184

At home
Look through your kitchen cupboards with your child. Can you find any 'clues' that tell you what is in each package and where it comes from (for example, wheat on a bag of flour).

Making food

Explore

a Say the number of cakes on each plate.
b Colour the cakes using 2 colours.

At home
Make or buy some plain cupcakes and decorate them with your child.

In this session, children will also: help make bread and learn about kneading, write a sentence about bread, create and play in a pretend bakery. → TG pp. 181–184

Making food

a Look. What is in each picture?

b Number the pictures in the right order.

In this session, children will also: help to make butter, find out about milk production in their region, use toy cows to practise placing numbers in order. → TG pp. 181–184

Explore

At home
Talk with your child about how some animals live in fields or on farms. If you have any farm animal toys, discuss what the animals eat. Explain that they also make food for us.

Making food

a Tick (✓) the fruit you like best.

b Colour the jar to show your jam.

At home
If possible, try different flavours of jam with your child. Talk about the different fruits used to make jam. Which flavour do they like best?

In this session, children will also: learn how to make jam, play a CVC word game, make up their own story with props, practise controlling and moving a ball. → TG pp. 181–184

Measure and mix

Explore

a Circle the full jar 🔴.
b Circle the lightest jar 🟢.

In this session, children will also: explore number bonds by sharing out pasta shapes, lift buckets to compare their weight, share recipe books. → TG pp. 185–188

At home
With your child, add dried foods (e.g. rice, pasta, dried pulses) to clean jam jars to make an 'instrument'. Shake your jars in different rhythmic patterns.

Measure and mix

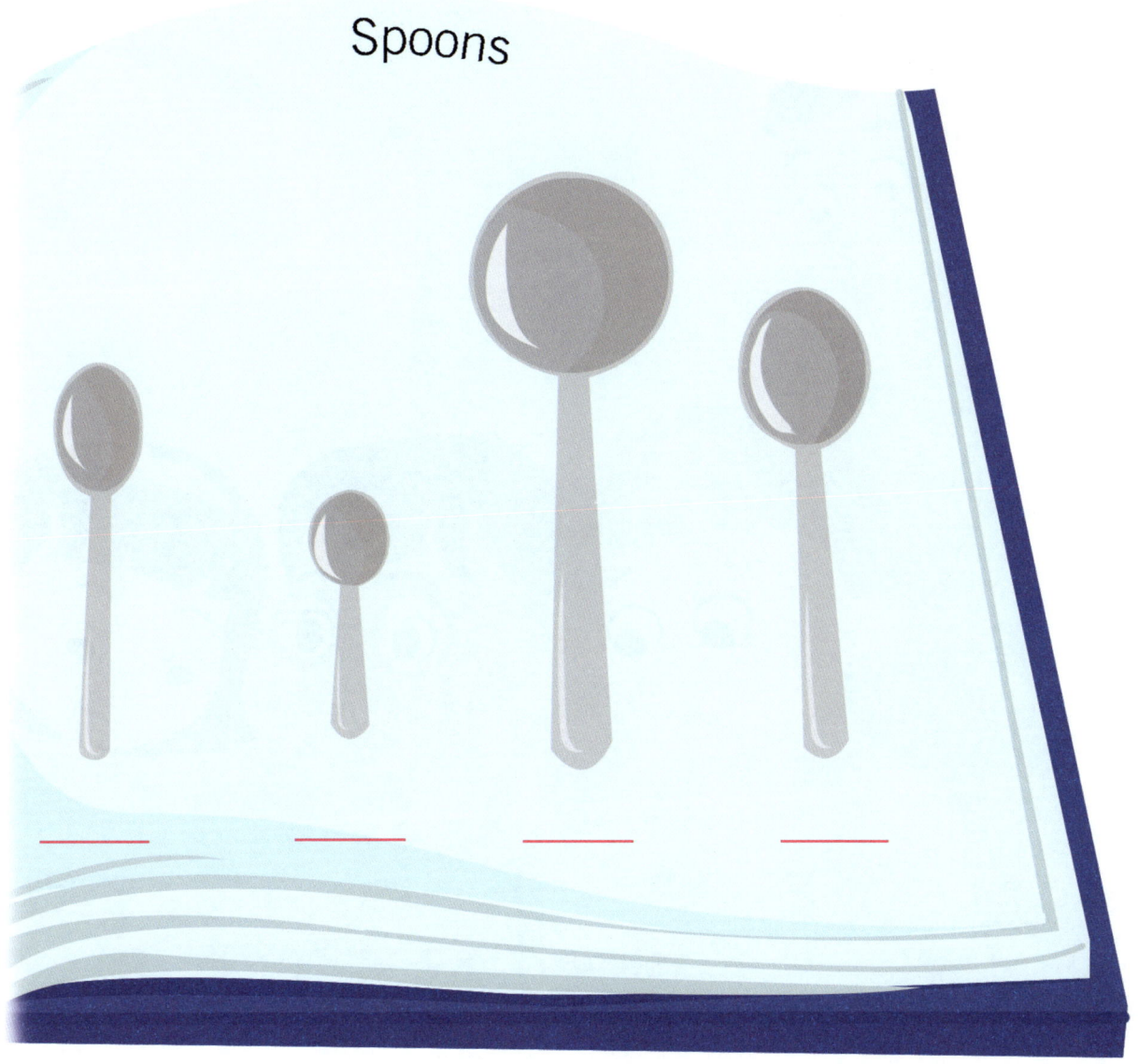

Explore

a Number the spoons in size order.
1 is the smallest.

c _____ _____ k   b _____ _____ k

f _____ _____ d

b Complete the words by adding 'oo'.

In this session, children will also: create their own recipes as they play in an outdoor kitchen, write simple recipes, experience sensory play with cornflour gloop. → TG pp. 185–188

At home
Ask your child to help you lay the table by setting out the cutlery, talking about what each item of cutlery is used for.

Measure and mix

Explore

a Count. How many ingredients are there?
b Look. What thing measures milk?
c Find the foods made by animals.

At home
Share recipe books with your child. Talk about the amounts of ingredients and the equipment used to measure them.

In this session, children will also: follow instructions and measure real ingredients to make 'overnight oats', talk about breakfast, take part in a water relay. → TG pp. 185–188

Measure and mix

Connect

a Look. What is happening?

b Tick (✓) what you need to go shopping.

At home
Go on a shopping trip with your child to buy ingredients for a meal.

In this session, children will also: talk about feeling cross and calming down, create and play in a pretend shop, play the 'shopping basket' memory game. → TG pp. 185–188

a Sing A favourite recipe.
b Find the steps to make the snack.
c Explain how to make the snack.
d Look. What are they cooking?

At home
Look at recipe books with your child. Talk about the different sections of a recipe (for example, ingredients and method). Select a recipe to make together.

In these sessions, children will also: choose ingredients for a snack, write a simple recipe, learn new words, make food models, talk about food from different places. → TG pp. 188–191

Favourite recipes

Explore

1 ___ ___ ___ ___

1 ___ ___ ___ ___ ___

1 ___ ___ ___

a Number the eggs in each row.
b Circle the row that has most eggs.

At home
When you are cooking, ask your child to help you count the number of each ingredient.

In this session, children will also: use a number grid to count to 20, create a pretend restaurant, make menus. → TG pp. 188–191

Favourite recipes

Explore

a Find the egg in each picture.

b Look. Which dish would you like to try?

At home
Talk with your child about how many dishes they can think of that contain eggs.

In this session, children will also: investigate eggs and the changes when cooked, learn about egg dishes from around the world, play games with a rugby ball. → TG pp. 188–191

Favourite recipes

a Tick (✓) the decorations on the cake.
b Say which decorations you like.

At home
Help your child decorate a small, plain cake or biscuit, using some different toppings.

In this session, children will also: help make and decorate butterfly cakes, observe cream changing when it is whisked, play a game about cake ingredients. → TG pp. 188–191

Let's all cook!

"I mix."

"I tip."

"Let's cook!"

Cakes

a Say the Let's all cook rhyme.
b Look. What rhymes with **cook**?
c Find the biggest and smallest cup.
d Count the tubes of icing.

At home
Choose an easy recipe that you can follow with your child. Take pictures or film the process!

In this session, children will also: make up a story about cooking cakes, say and write strings of rhyming words, join in with rhymes and songs about food. → TG pp. 192–194

Let's all cook!

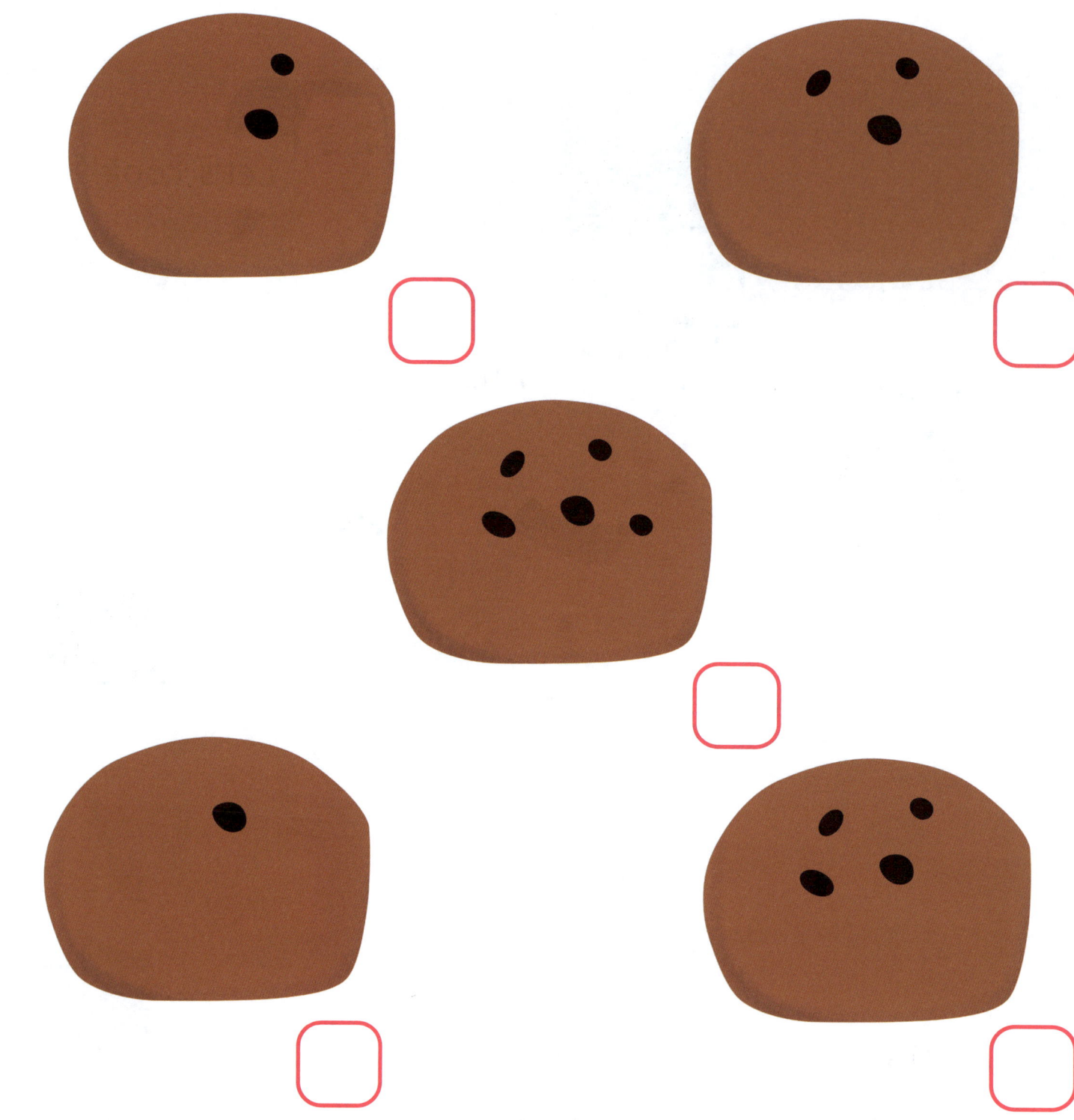

a Say the number of currants on each bun.

b Tick (✓) the bun with the most currants.

At home

Ask your child to count the chocolate chips on a cookie. Compare 2 cookies: which has the most chocolate chips on top?

In this session, children will also: sing 'Five currant buns', find out about currants, share and compare different quantities, develop the role-play restaurant. → TG pp. 192–194

Let's all cook!

a Look. Which plate has the most food?
b Say which foods you like to eat.

In this session, children will also: use their senses to describe fruit and vegetables, make rainbow wraps, collect different coloured items in an active game. → TG pp. 192–194

At home
Talk about the colours of foods in your home with your child, for example, the fruits in your fruit bowl.

Let's all cook!

Explore

a Colour the carrot ice cream.

b Think. Would you like carrot ice cream?

At home
Sing a rhyme about food with your child, for example, 'Pat-a-cake' or 'Little Miss Muffet'.

Let's all cook!

brown

orange

purple

green

blue

Review

a Say what colours you can see.
b Match the colours.

In this session, children will also: write a short phrase about their favourite recipe, use tweezers to pick up and sort small coloured objects, compare quantities. → TG pp. 192–194

At home
With your child, practise singing 'I can sing a rainbow'.

Rain or shine

In this topic, learners are encouraged to:
- learn how plants change between seasons
- understand how the weather is measured
- discuss storm safety and types of storm
- count beyond 20 with help and compare amounts
- think about weather using their senses
- reflect on how to enjoy different weather.

Teachers will also help learners to:
- plant and grow a sunflower
- create their own weather station
- use the internet to see weather in other places
- explore natural materials like mud and ice
- use number lines and explore cardinality.

Super seasons

Gibran's garden

a Name the seasons in the pictures. Which one is missing?

b Retell the story.

At home
Talk about the seasons. Ask your child to think of one simple describing word (adjective) for each one.

In this session, children will also: look at plant bulbs; learn about calendars, months, seasons; observe changing seasons; learn time adjectives; make art inspired by flowers. → TG pp. 195–198

Super seasons

Explore

a Tick (✓) the 2 buckets that have 12 flowers altogether.

b Colour all the flowers.

At home
Arrange some flowers with your child. If you have a garden or window box, your child could pick flowers themselves, or choose some in a shop.

In this session, children will also: explore different ways to make 12, label the parts of a flower, create a pretend flower stall. → TG pp. 195–198

Super seasons

a Number the plants in order from youngest to oldest.

b Circle the plant with the most leaves.

In this session, children will also: think about how plants grow over time, practise counting one more or one less than a number, make giant flower shapes outside. → TG pp. 195–198

At home
Try planting and growing some seeds with your child. Big seeds, for example, sunflower seeds or pumpkin seeds are easy to handle and plant individually.

Super seasons

a Look. Which season is it?

b Colour the autumn leaves.

In this session, children will also: share stories about kindness. think about practical ways to be kind, make crowns with natural objects, take part in 1-minute challenges. → TG pp. 195–198

At home
With your child, look for simple shapes in nature, for example different-shaped petals and leaves.

Changing weather

"Look!"

a Look. What is the weather like?
b Count the leaves above Gibran.
c Say who is measuring rainfall.
d Find the tool for measuring wind.

At home
Go outside with your child on a windy day. Look for things being blown about by the wind, for example, leaves, clothes, and people's hair.

In this session, children will also: make observations of the weather, write a sentence about the day's weather, pretend to be TV weather forecasters. → TG pp. 199–202

Changing weather

big clouds _____   small clouds _____

total clouds _____

a Count and write the numbers.

At home
Go outside and lie down in a green space like a garden or park with your child. Use your imagination and talk about what the clouds look like.

Changing weather

 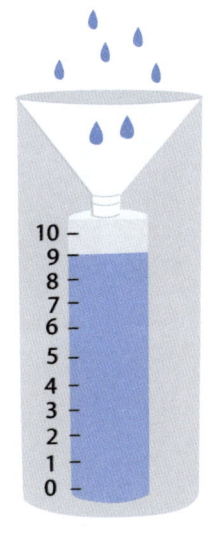

nearly full   half-full   full

a Match the rain gauges to how full they are.

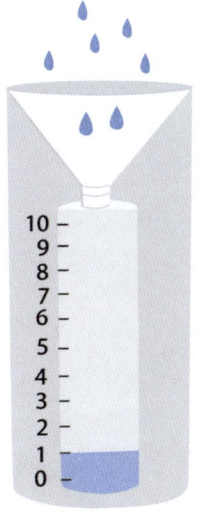 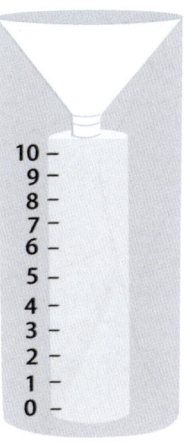

b Circle the gauge with no water.

At home
Make a simple rain gauge with your child. Use a plastic bottle and write numbers on the side in permanent marker. Leave it outside and check it regularly.

In this session, children will also: compare the capacity of different containers, practise moving buckets of water, play a counting steps game. → TG pp. 199–202

Changing weather

a Look. What makes the windmills move?

b Colour in your own windmill.

At home

Check the weather conditions for the day. Talk with your child about the most appropriate clothing to wear outside.

Changing weather

1

a Number the sticks.

b Say how many sticks are blank.

1 = 🔴   2 = 🟠

c Colour the blank sticks by number.

At home
With your child, look for items that make a noise when they blow in the wind. If there are any wind chimes around, listen to the sounds they make.

In this session, children will also: make wind chimes, listen and respond to music, play an active game. → TG pp. 199–202

a Sing The storm song.
b Say how the children feel.
c Count the people in Tarek's family.
d Find all the torches.

At home
With your child, think about what things make them feel calm and safe during bad weather. Make a list with words and drawings.

In these sessions, children will also: talk about feeling scared, investigate torches, find out about thunderstorms, play a number track game, create their own dens. → TG pp. 202–205

Storms

Explore

a Write the number of raindrops.
b Colour the cloud with most raindrops.

At home
Sing the simple nursery rhyme 'Rain, rain, go away' with your child when it rains.

In this session, children will also: look at storms in art, create a storm collage, learn clapping games. → TG pp. 202–205

Storms

a Look. Make the sounds you might hear.

b Tick (✓) the quietest sound.

At home
Talk with your child about the noises you hear when it is stormy. Discuss any special safety precautions for certain weather in your area.

In this session, children will also: make storm sounds with instruments and other materials, learn about extreme storms, practice safety procedures. → TG pp. 202–205

Storms

a Colour what keeps us dry.

Storms make me feel …

_____

b Write how storms make you feel.

In this session, children will also: sing and dance to weather songs, make up a story about being out in the rain, play a game with actions for weather. → TG pp. 202–205

At home
Talk with your child about how the weather can make us feel and what we should do to stay safe.

Weather play

a Say the Weather play poem.
b Look. What do you like doing?
c Count the children.
d Find things we wear or use in the rain.

At home
Ask your child to finish the sentence: 'When it is rainy, I like to...' Repeat for sunny, windy, and snowy weather.

In this session, children will also: choose activities to do in different weathers, create and play in a mud kitchen. → TG pp. 206–208

Weather play

a Tick (✓) the things the boy needs for a rainy day.

b Find the thing that rhymes with **map**.

At home
Give your child paper and pens, and ask them to draw a picture of themselves outside on a rainy day. What clothes would they be wearing?

Weather play

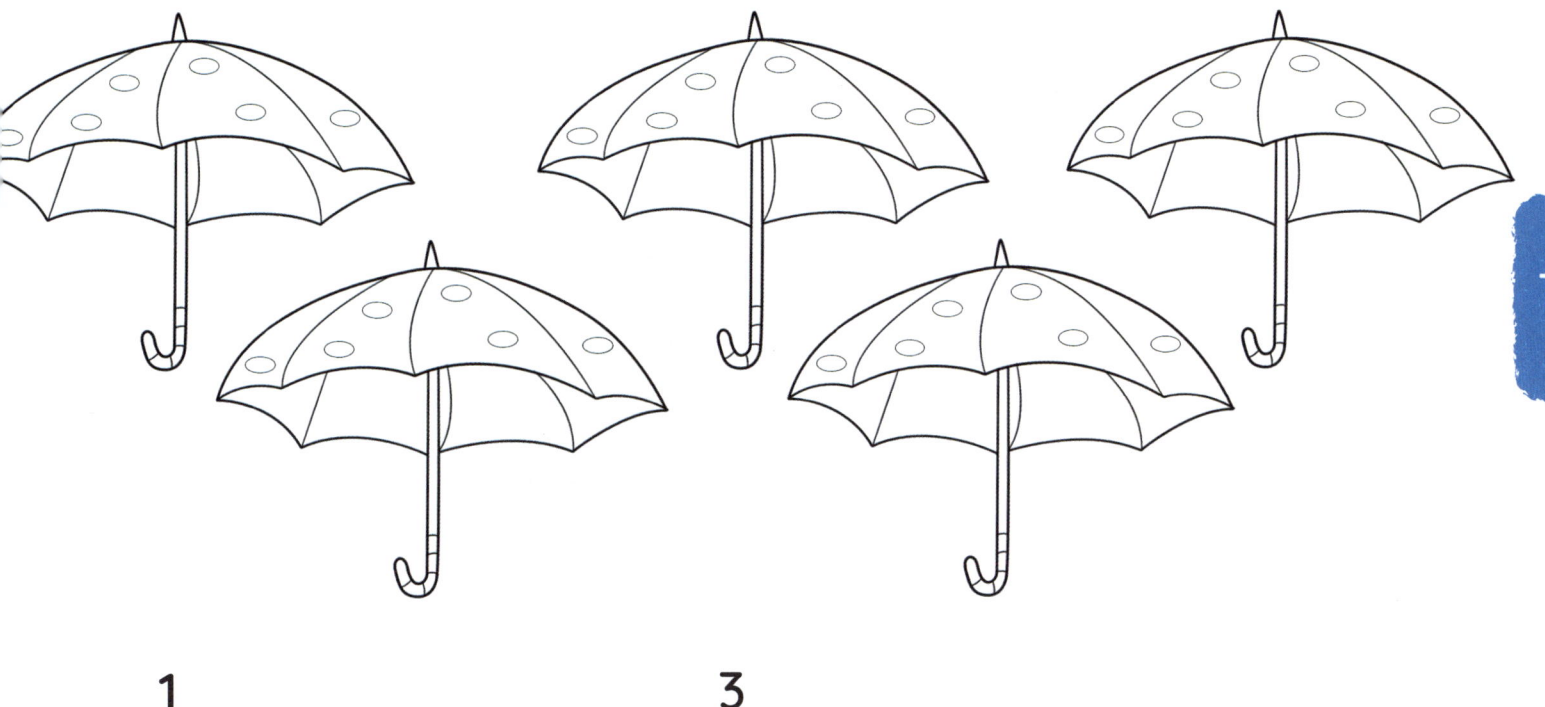

_____ 1 _____ _____ 3 _____ _____

_____ 6 _____ _____ _____ _____

a Write the missing numbers.

b Listen to your teacher and colour the umbrellas.

At home
Ask your child to help you sort or fold the laundry. Talk about the different types of clothing we wear for different weather, and why.

In this session, children will also: look at kites flying, make and test sailing boats, place items to match the numerals on a number line. → TG pp. 206–208

Weather play

Explore

a Circle the children who are playing.

hot   cold

b Trace the word that describes snow.

At home
Talk with your child about all the fun things you can do in snow.

In this session, children will also: find out about living in very cold temperatures, make predictions and observe ice melting, practise moving in different ways. → TG pp. 206–208

Weather play

- sunny

rainy -

a Match the weather to its picture.
b Colour the weather you prefer to play in.

At home
Before your child gets out of bed or looks outside, ask them to predict what the weather will be like. Or mime what the weather is and ask them to guess.

In this session, children will also review their learning by: writing a sentence about the weather, completing a 0–20 number line, practise naming flower parts. → TG pp. 206–208

Growing and changing

In this topic, learners are encouraged to:
- study a well-known fairy tale
- find different shapes in the world around them
- understand how plants grow
- understand the human life cycle
- compare heights and ages.

Teachers will also help learners to:
- plant and grow beans
- retell a story
- use a variety of items to make measurements
- understand their own development
- learn about animals and their babies.

Getting bigger

Tarek's beanstalk

a Listen to your teacher and count the things.

b Retell the story.

At home
Talk about the story of 'Jack and the Beanstalk' with your child and help them retell it. You can find videos and retellings of the story online.

In this session, children will also: predict a story ending, count 20 beans, create and play in a 'Tarek's beanstalk' role-play area. → TG pp. 209–212

Getting bigger

a Write the number of leaves on each beanstalk.

1	2	3	4	5
6	7	8	9	10
11	12	13	14	15
16	17	18	19	20

b Circle the total number of leaves.

At home
With your child, look for seedlings in the garden or a nearby green space. Help your child observe what happens as the seedlings grow.

Getting bigger

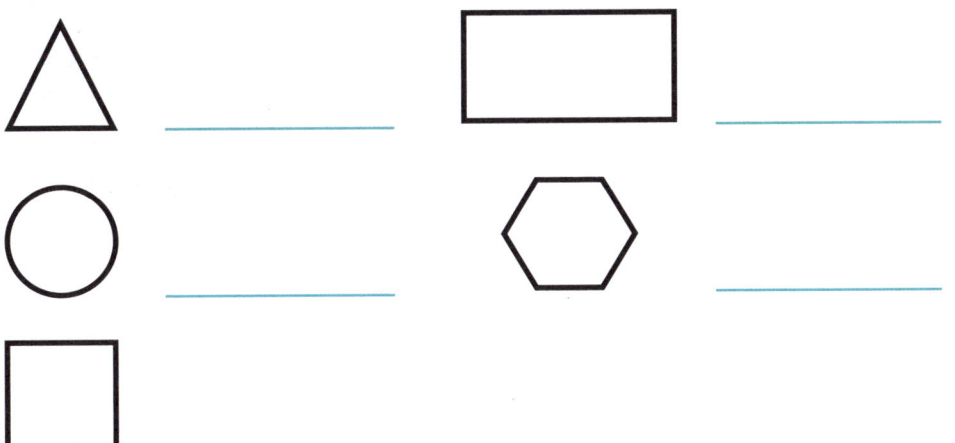

a Colour each shape in the tower a different colour.

b Write the total number of each shape.

At home
Share some traditional tales at bedtime with your child. Talk about the different stories and find out which one is their favourite and why.

In this session, children will also: work as a team to help build a giant's castle out of boxes, practise moving like a giant, help draw a giant in the playground. → TG pp. 209–212

Getting bigger

a Say what is happening in the picture.

- goat
- crab
- snail
- bird

b Match the shadow animals to their names.

c Are the shadows bigger or smaller than the hands?

At home
With your child, make shadows using small toys and a lamp, a torch, or the sun for a source of light. You could put paper beneath the shadows and ask your child to draw around them.

In this session, children will also: observe shadows and how to make them bigger, count in 2s along a number track, make towers that get 'one higher' each time. → TG pp. 209–212

Getting bigger

a Look. Who is Sam pretending to be?

b Name the shapes in the tower.

c Count the squares.

In this session, children will also: observe bean seeds growing, play a 'giant footsteps' game, talk about ways to solve problems, practise making different shapes. ➜ TG pp. 209–212

At home
Help your child look for different shapes in the world around them.

a Sing the Plant and grow song.
b Find 2 things that plants need to grow.
c Trace the snail's trail with a finger.
d Look. Which are the tallest flowers?

At home
Print pictures of flowers or find some in a magazine. Help your child cut them out and make a pretty collage-bouquet on a piece of paper.

In these sessions, children will also: act and use action words linked to gardening, trace a line through a maze, plan a class garden project, look at the parts of a bean plant. → TG pp. 213–215

Plants grow too!

a Look. Say which is the tallest.

b Add numbers in size order: 1 is tallest.

At home
Take a walk with your child and spot the plants that are growing, talking about which ones are tallest and shortest.

In this session, children will also: measure themselves against plants outside, investigate a metre rule, work on the class garden project. → TG pp. 213–215

Plants grow too!

a Trace the numbers.
   Match to show the right order.

b Colour the natural things.

At home
Look at different plants in your kitchen (fruits, vegetables, herbs) with your child. Discuss the parts we eat, for example the leaves of a lettuce or the root of ginger.

In this session, children will also: plant bean seedlings, find out what happens to bean plants as they grow, add flowers and plants to the class garden project. → TG pp. 213–215

Plants grow too!

a Look. Which plant is shorter than Rani?
b Tick (✓) the plant that is taller than her.
c Find the plant that is the same size as her.

At home
With your child, compare the sizes of objects around the home. For example, a pencil might be the same length as your child's hand or the same height as a plant.

Growing up

a Find the oldest and youngest person.
b Look. Who is the tallest?
c Count the kittens.
d Compare. Who looks most like their picture?

At home
Show your child pictures of them and of you as a baby. Compare the pictures. Talk about similarities and differences.

In this session, children will also: talk about their own families, look at baby photos and talk about change, pretend to look after babies in the home corner. → TG pp. 216–218

Growing up

Explore

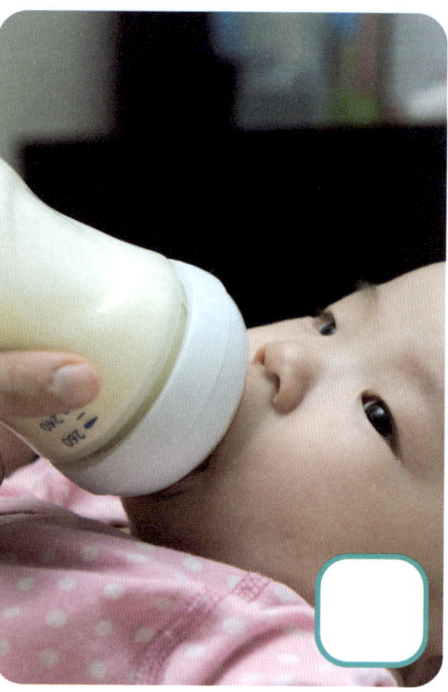

a Look. Which things do you do?

b Cross (✗) the things babies can't do.

In this session, children will also: look at a timeline of 0–5 milestones, say and write about their baby photo, practise numbers bonds to 12, meet an older family member. → TG pp. 216–218

At home
Look at items from when your child was a baby, for example, their first drinking cup, a sleepsuit, a first toy. Talk with your child about how they are different now.

Growing up

a Add the pattern on the other wing.
b Colour to make a matching pattern.

At home
Look for things that are the same on both sides, like butterflies. Reinforce the words 'symmetry' and 'symmetrical' with your child.

In this session, children will also: review a butterfly lifecycle, compare the human lifecycle, practise adding matching pairs of numbers, learn about other lifecycles. → TG pp. 216–218

Growing up

Explore

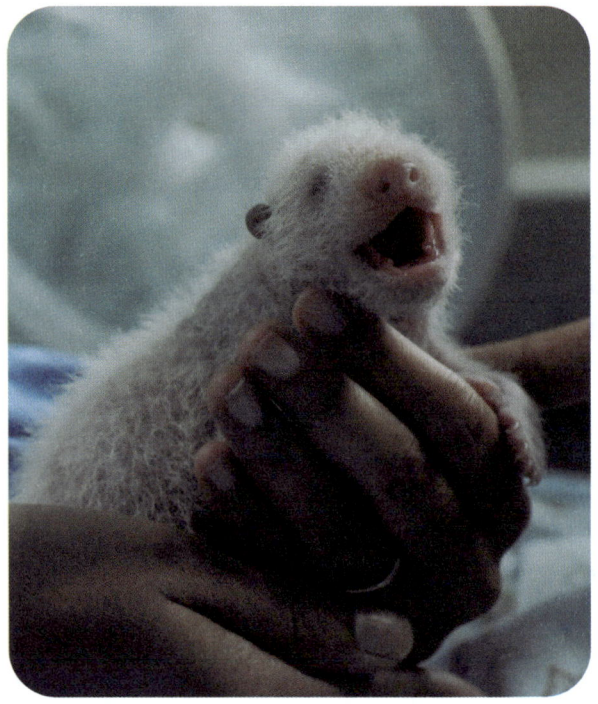

adult baby

a Say how the animals are the same and how they are different.

b Trace the words.

c Match the words to the pictures.

At home
Use the internet or books with your child to find out how animals change into adulthood.

In this session, children will also: compare timelines for a panda and a human baby, share stories about animals and their babies, complete an obstacle course. → TG pp. 216–218

Growing up

a Colour the markings on the adults.

b Look at the markings. Are their shapes familiar?

At home
Talk with your child about the shapes they can find in their toys and in their bedroom.

In this session, children will also: find out about animal camouflage, talk about what children need to help them grow, practise counting in 2s and 5s, play using camouflage. → TG pp. 216–218

a Say the Let's measure rhyme.
b Look. Where are Rani's family today?
c Count the measuring tools.
d Find all the living things.

At home

With your child, use a non-standard measuring tool (like your child's handspan or a pencil) to measure items around the house. For example: 'This chair is 12 pencils high.'

Let's measure!

Explore

a Count the measuring tools.
b Colour the lightest bucket 🟦.
c Colour the heaviest bucket 🟥.

At home
Go around your home with your child, identifying all the things you have that measure things (e.g. cooking scales, rulers, clocks, jugs, etc.).

In this session, children will also: name different measuring tools and find out how to use them, predict and compare capacity, practise using a bucket balance. → TG pp. 219–221

Let's measure!

a Find the smallest elephant.

b Tick (✓) the elephant with tusks.

c Look. How is the baby elephant different?

In this session, children will also: measure how far they can jump, use a timer to compare how long they take to run or hop, make the biggest elephant model. → TG pp. 219–221

At home
With your child, talk about when they were a baby. Share stories about how they learned to talk or walk.

Let's measure!

a Find the youngest and oldest person.

b Look. Which plant is the youngest? Which plant is the tallest?

At home

Ask your child to compare the heights and ages of people in the family. Who is shorter, taller, older, or younger than them?